On Love & Marriage

Edited by
Nick Beilenson

With Illustrations by
Wendy Watson

Designed by
Rachael A. Peden

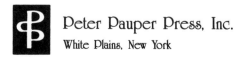
Peter Pauper Press, Inc.
White Plains, New York

For this edition, the compilation of Robert J. Myers has been edited by Nick Beilenson.

A COLLECTION OF
WITTY SAYINGS
FOR AND AGAINST THE
PROFANE STATE OF
LOVE AND THE
HOLY STATE OF MATRIMONY

On Love and Marriage

Love, the quest; marriage, the conquest;
divorce, the inquest.

HELEN ROWLAND

All the world loves a lover, except those
who are waiting to use the phone.

A gentleman who had been very
unhappy in marriage married
immediately after his wife died: Johnson
said it was the triumph of hope over
experience.

JAMES BOSWELL

Were kisses all the joys in bed,
One woman would another wed.

WILLIAM SHAKESPEARE

After all these years, I see that I was mistaken about Eve in the beginning; it is better to live outside the Garden with her than inside it without her.

MARK TWAIN

Brigands demand your money or your life; women require both.

SAMUEL BUTLER

Love is an archer with a low I.Q.

PHYLLIS McGINLEY

The most happy marriage I can picture . . . would be the union of a deaf man to a blind woman.

SAMUEL COLERIDGE

Thy wife is a constellation of virtues; she's the moon, and thou art the man in the moon.

WILLIAM CONGREVE

If a man cannot distinguish the difference between the pleasures of two consecutive nights, he has married too early in life.

HONORÉ DE BALZAC

A happy man marries the girl he loves, but a happier man loves the girl he marries.

Nobody works as hard for his money as the man who married it.

KIN HUBBARD

Men seldom make passes
At girls who wear glasses.

DOROTHY PARKER

When a man finds a beautiful girl and a good housewife he may have a perfect marriage, but it sounds like bigamy.

UNKNOWN

I feel sorry for young women. They are living in a frenetic atmosphere, which is a hazard to friendship, to courtship and certainly to what should be the calm decision to marry.

MARY LEE SETTLE

Forty years of romance make a woman look like a ruin and forty years of marriage make her look like a public building.

OSCAR WILDE

Marriage is a gamble—that's why we speak of winning a husband or wife.

Marriage, in life, is like a duel in the midst of a battle.

EDMOND ABOUT

The trouble with matrimony is not with the institution, it's with the personnel.

They stood before the altar and supplied
The fire themselves in which their fat
    was fried.

AMBROSE BIERCE

To marry a woman or man for beauty is
like buying a house for its coat of paint.

AMERICAN PROVERB

The only merit of some women is to
excite; of others, to satisfy.

AMIS

To be a woman is to have the same
needs and longings as a man. We need
love and we wish to give it.

LIV ULLMANN

If you want peace in your house, do as
your wife wants.

AFRICAN PROVERB

It is a truth universally acknowledged that a single man in possession of a good fortune must be in want of a wife.

JANE AUSTEN

It is always incomprehensible to a man that a woman should refuse an offer of marriage.

JANE AUSTEN

Wives are young men's mistresses, companions for middle age, and old men's nurses.

FRANCIS BACON

A man's mother is his misfortune, but his wife is his fault.

WALTER BAGEHOT

A sweetheart is a bottle of wine, a wife is a wine bottle.

CHARLES BAUDELAIRE

Marriage: the state or condition of a community consisting of a master, a mistress and two slaves, making in all, two.

AMBROSE BIERCE

Woman would be more charming if one could fall into her arms without falling into her hands.

AMBROSE BIERCE

Money cannot buy love, but it can put you in a good bargaining position.

Love-matches are made by people who are content, for a month of honey, to condemn themselves to a life of vinegar.

COUNTESS OF BLESSINGTON

One should always be in love. That is the reason one should never marry.

OSCAR WILDE

How do I love thee? Let me count the
  ways.
I love thee to the depth and breadth and
  height
My soul can reach, when feeling out of
  sight
For the ends of Being, and Ideal Grace.
I love thee to the level of every day's
Most quiet need, by sun and candle-
  light.
I love thee freely as men strive for Right;
I love thee purely as they turn from
  Praise;
I love thee with the passion put to use
In my old griefs and with my
  childhood's faith;
I love thee with a love I seemed to lose
With my lost saints,—I love thee with
  the breath,
Smiles, tears, of all my life! And, if God
  choose,
I shall but love thee better after death.

ELIZABETH BARRETT BROWNING

No cord or cable can draw so forcibly, or bind so fast, as love can do with a single thread.

ROBERT BURTON

Every man, as the saying is, can tame a shrew but he that hath her.

ROBERT BURTON

Matrimony and bachelorhood are both of them at once equally wise and equally foolish.

SAMUEL BUTLER

Love is an attempt at penetrating another being, but it can only succeed if the surrender is mutual.

OCTAVIO PAZ

All tragedies are finish'd by a death,
    All comedies are ended by a marriage.

LORD BYRON

There's nothing in the world like the devotion of a married woman. It's a thing no married man knows anything about.

OSCAR WILDE

Love doesn't grow on trees like apples in Eden—it's something you have to make. And you must use your imagination too. . . .

JOYCE CARY

A poor beauty finds more lovers than husbands.

ENGLISH PROVERB

After your fling, watch for the sting.

ENGLISH PROVERB

Marriage, as practiced by high society, is arranged indecency.

NICHOLAS CHAMFORT

If you are afraid of loneliness, don't
marry.

ANTON CHEKHOV

The only solid and lasting peace,
between a man and his wife, is,
doubtless, a separation.

LORD CHESTERFIELD

Other men's wives are always the best.

CHINESE PROVERB

What? Rise again with *all* one's bones?
    Quoth Giles, I hope you fib.
I trusted when I went to Heaven
    To go without my rib.

S. T. COLERIDGE

Love pleases more than marriage, for the
reason that romance is more interesting
than history.

NICHOLAS CHAMFORT

If a man stay away from his wife for seven years, the law presumes the separation to have killed him; yet, according to our daily experience, it might well prolong his life.

C. J. DARLING

In Paris, when God provides a beautiful woman, the devil at once retorts with a fool to keep her.

BARBEY D'AUREVILLY

For lovers, touch is metamorphosis. All the parts of their bodies seem to change, and they become something different and better.

JOHN CHEEVER

In the limitless desert of love, sensual pleasure has an ardent but very small place, so incandescent that at first one sees nothing else.

COLETTE

Marriage is a feast where the grace is sometimes better than the dinner.

C. C. COLTON

Every man plays the fool once in his life, but to marry is playing the fool all one's life long.

WILLIAM CONGREVE

The two happiest moments in the lives of a married couple are when the clergyman marries them and the judge divorces them.

To a woman at 18 marriage is an adventure, at 22 a career, at 30 a goal, and at 40 a haven.

The one charm of marriage is that it makes a life of deception absolutely necessary for both parties.

OSCAR WILDE

When a woman marries again it is because she detested her first husband. When a man marries again, it is because he adored his first wife. Women try their luck; men risk theirs.

Oscar Wilde

Squeeze marriage as much as you like, you will never extract anything from it but fun for bachelors and boredom for husbands.

Honoré de Balzac

The woman who is about to deceive her husband always carefully thinks out how she is going to act, but she is never logical.

Honoré de Balzac

A woman who has once laughed at her husband can no longer love him.

Honoré de Balzac

I have found it impossible to carry the heavy burden of responsibility and to discharge my duties as King as I would wish to do without the help and support of the woman I love.

EDWARD, DUKE OF WINDSOR

A husband and wife who are in the habit of occupying separate rooms are either beings apart, or they have found happiness. Either they hate or they adore each other.

HONORÉ DE BALZAC

Generally speaking, women like to live fast, but after the storms in their feelings come the calms that are so reassuring to the husband's happiness.

HONORÉ DE BALZAC

A fool and his money are soon married.

To love someone means to see him as
God intended him.

DOSTOEVSKI

Your wife feels towards the pleasures of
marriage like a Mohican would feel at
the Opera: the interpreter is annoyed
when the savage begins to understand.

HONORÉ DE BALZAC

Love is a power too strong to be
overcome by anything but flight.

MIGUEL DE CERVANTES

Mourning the loss of someone we love is
happiness compared with having to live
with someone we hate.

JEAN DE LA BRUYÈRE

It is too severe on a husband for a
woman to be given both to flirtation and
devotion; she should make her choice.

JEAN DE LA BRUYÈRE

When one has once fully entered the realm of love, the world—no matter how imperfect—becomes rich and beautiful, for it consists solely of opportunities for love.

SOREN KIERKEGAARD

Alas! though we burn with desire
    without measure
Modesty robs us of all of love's pleasure.

MADAME DE LA SUZE

Marriage is like a cage; one sees the birds outside desperate to get in, and those inside equally desperate to get out.

MICHEL DE MONTAIGNE

A good marriage, if there is such a thing, rejects the company and conditions of love. It tries to imitate those of friendship.

MICHEL DE MONTAIGNE

The concern that some women show at the absence of their husbands does not arise from their not seeing them and being with them, but from the apprehension that their husbands are enjoying pleasures in which they do not participate, and which, from their being at a distance, they have not the power of interrupting.

MICHEL DE MONTAIGNE

Marriage, a market which has nothing free but the entrance.

MICHEL DE MONTAIGNE

It is not you I love. I love to love as I love you. I am not counting on anything from you, my beloved. I expect nothing of you save my love for you.

ANNA DE NOAILLES

Every couple is not a pair.

ENGLISH PROVERB

"Going to him! Happy letter! Tell him—
Tell him the page I didn't write;
Tell him I only said the syntax,
And left the verb and pronoun out."

EMILY DICKINSON

We are born for love. It is the principle
of existence and its only end.

BENJAMIN DISRAELI

Every man should marry—and no
woman.

BENJAMIN DISRAELI

A man does not look behind the door
unless he has stood there himself.

HENRI DU BOIS

Women are never stronger than when
they arm themselves with their
weakness.

MADAME DU DEFFAND

It is not true that love makes all things easy; it makes us choose what is difficult.

GEORGE ELIOT

All mankind loves a lover.

RALPH WALDO EMERSON

Who marrieth for love without money hath good nights and sorry days.

ENGLISH PROVERB

Marriage halves our griefs, doubles our joys, and quadruples our expenses.

ENGLISH PROVERB

Whoever said marriage is a fifty-fifty proposition doesn't know the half of it.

Take heed of a widow thrice married.

ENGLISH PROVERB

One can always recognize women who trust their husbands. They look so thoroughly unhappy.

OSCAR WILDE

A man can be happy with any woman as long as he does not love her.

OSCAR WILDE

All are good lasses, but whence come the bad wives?

ENGLISH PROVERB

It's a good horse that never stumbles,
And a good wife that never grumbles.

ENGLISH PROVERB

First we make up, and then we fight:
    (A miserable wretch am I!)
To live with her's beyond me quite,
    And yet without her I should die.

JEAN DESMARETS

Who has not found the heaven below
    Will fail of it above.
God's residence is next to mine,
    His furniture is love.

EMILY DICKINSON

So heavy is the chain of wedlock that it
needs two to carry it, and sometimes
three.

ALEXANDRE DUMAS

When widows exclaim loudly against
second marriages, I would always lay a
wager that the man, if not the wedding
day, is absolutely fixed on.

HENRY FIELDING

Love preserves beauty, and the flesh of
woman is fed with caresses as are bees
with flowers.

ANATOLE FRANCE

Where there's marriage without love,
there will be love without marriage.

BENJAMIN FRANKLIN

Are women books? says Hodge, then
would mine were an Almanack, to
change her every year.

BENJAMIN FRANKLIN

One good Husband is worth two good
wives, for the scarcer things are the
more they're valued.

BENJAMIN FRANKLIN

Grief often treads upon the heels of
  pleasure,
Marry'd in haste, we oft repent at
  leisure;
Some by experience find these words
  misplaced,
Marry'd at leisure, they repent in haste.

BENJAMIN FRANKLIN

Here's to matrimony, the high sea for which no compass has yet been invented.

HEINRICH HEINE

He that tells his wife news is but newly married.

GEORGE HERBERT

Kissing and bussing differ in this:
We busse our Wantons, but our Wives
we kisse.

ROBERT HERRICK

The most precious possession that ever comes to a man in this world is a woman's heart.

HOLLAND

Love is the master key that opens the gates of happiness.

OLIVER WENDELL HOLMES

I should like to see any kind of a man, distinguishable from a gorilla, that some good and even pretty woman could not shape a husband out of.

OLIVER WENDELL HOLMES

You can bear your own Faults, and why not a Fault in a Wife?

BENJAMIN FRANKLIN

Do you think your mother and I should have liv'd comfortably so long together, if ever we had been married?

JOHN GAY

Love is the last and most serious of the diseases of childhood.

Generally the woman chooses the man who will choose her.

GERALDY

Love often leads to marriage—and almost as often to divorce.

Keep your eyes wide open before marriage, and half-shut afterwards.

BENJAMIN FRANKLIN

Easy-crying widows take new husbands soonest; there is nothing like wet weather for transplanting, as Master Gridley used to say.

OLIVER WENDELL HOLMES

Experience teaches us that love does not consist of two people looking at each other, but of looking together in the same direction.

ANTOINE DE SAINT-EXUPERY

Marriage is legalized prostitution.

CLAIRE DEMAR

A good and true woman is said to resemble a Cremona fiddle—age but increases its worth and sweetens its tone.

OLIVER WENDELL HOLMES

When the wife makes the husband rich, there's the devil in the house.

GERMAN PROVERB

Wives and watermelons are picked by chance.

GREEK PROVERB

The feller that puts off marryin' till he can support a wife ain't very much in love.

KIN HUBBARD

Married life hain't so bad after you git so you kin eat th' things your wife likes.

KIN HUBBARD

Life is a flower of which love is the honey.

VICTOR HUGO

A man should be taller, older, heavier, uglier and hoarser than his wife.

E. W. HOWE

There is only one thing for a man to do who is married to a woman who enjoys spending money, and that is to enjoy earning it.

E. W. HOWE

A foolish girl may make a lover a husband, but it takes a clever woman to keep a husband a lover.

ED HOWE

Who marries well does well, who marries not does better.

JAMES HOWELL

In love all of life's contradictions dissolve and disappear. Only in love are unity and duality not in conflict.

RABINDRANATH TAGORE

When Eve upon the first of men
    The apple pressed with specious cant,
Oh, what a thousand pities then
    That Adam was not *Adamant!*

THOMAS HOOD

A man who married a woman to educate her falls into the same fallacy as the woman who marries a man to reform him.

ELBERT HUBBARD

The supreme happiness of life is the conviction of being loved for yourself, or, more correctly, being loved in spite of yourself.

VICTOR HUGO

When a woman ceases to be mistress of herself she is likely to become the mistress of a man.

JAMES G. HUNEKER

Choose in marriage only a woman whom you would choose as a friend if she were a man.

JOUBERT

The better the man, the more desirable as a husband, the less good will he get out of his wife.

JUVENAL

There's no effrontery like that of a woman caught in the act.

JUVENAL

A wise lover values not so much the gift of the lover as the love of the giver.

THOMAS à KEMPIS

Love is never lost. If not reciprocated, it will flow back and soften and purify the heart.

WASHINGTON IRVING

The surest way to hit a woman's heart is to take aim kneeling.

DOUGLAS JERROLD

I believe it will be found that those who marry late are best pleased with their children, and those who marry early, with their partners.

SAMUEL JOHNSON

Every man gets the wife he deserves.

SIMEON B. LAKISH

Nature meant woman to be her masterpiece.

LESSING

Marriage by its best title is a monopoly.

CHARLES LAMB

A husband risks nothing in pretending
to believe that his wife is faithful, or in
silently assuming an air of patient
resignation. Silence worries a woman
more than anything.

HONORÉ DE BALZAC

Marriage always begins with a small
payment to a minister and often ends
with a large payment to a lawyer.

It is pleasant at times for a man to have
a jealous wife: there is constant mention
of what he loves.

LA ROCHEFOUCAULD

By biting and scratching cats and dogs
come together.

LATIN PROVERB

Nothing proves better the necessity of an indissoluble marriage than the instability of passion.

HONORÉ DE BALZAC

I have now come to the conclusion never again to think of marrying, and for this reason: I can never be satisfied with anyone who would be blockhead enough to have me.

ABRAHAM LINCOLN

Here lies my dear wife, a sad slattern
  and shrew;
If I said I regretted her, I should lie too.

H. J. LOARING

One of the main conveniences of marriage is that if you can't stand a visitor you can pass him along to your wife.

G. C. LICHTENBERG

One can, to an almost laughable degree, infer what a man's life is like from his opinions about women in general.

JOHN STUART MILL

Marriage is three parts love and seven parts forgiveness of sins.

LANGDON MITCHELL

'Tis the established custom (in Vienna) for every lady to have two husbands, one that bears the name and another that performs the duties.

MARY WORTLEY MONTAGU

If there were no husbands, who would look after our mistresses?

GEORGE MOORE

Where there is room in the heart, there is always room in the house.

THOMAS MOORE

The average woman must inevitably view her actual husband with a certain disdain; he is anything but her ideal. In consequence, she cannot help feeling that her children are cruelly handicapped by the fact that he is their father.

H. L. MENCKEN

Kissing don't last: cookery do!

GEORGE MEREDITH

There is nothing holier in this life of ours than the first consciousness of love—the first fluttering of its silken wings—the first rising sound and breath of that wind which is so soon to sweep through the soul.

HENRY WADSWORTH LONGFELLOW

After you have been married five years, there should always be someone to dinner.

EDWARD LUCAS

"Come, come," said Tom's father, "at
    your time of life,
    There's no longer excuse for thus
        playing the rake—
It is time you should think, boy, of
    taking a wife"—
    "Why, so it is, father—whose wife
        shall I take?"

THOMAS MOORE

There is no greater misfortune for a man
than to be governed by his wife: in such
a case he is neither himself nor his wife,
he is a perfect nonentity.

NAPOLEON I

We might knit that knot with our
tongues, that we shall never undo with
our teeth.

JOHN LYLY

Love gives itself; it is not bought.

HENRY WADSWORTH LONGFELLOW

At the beginning of a marriage ask yourself whether this woman will be interesting to talk to from now until old age. Everything else in marriage is transitory: most of the time is spent in conversation.

FRIEDRICH NIETZSCHE

The number of the Sacraments they fix
At seven, but, with the Pope's
   permission,
I should prefer to call them six,
For only one are marriage and contrition.

PANANTI

Strange to say what delight we married people have to see these poor fools decoyed into our condition.

SAMUEL PEPYS

He who would wed is marching toward repentance.

PHILEMON

A Roman divorced from his wife, being highly blamed by his friends, who demanded, "Was she not chaste? Was she not fair? Was she not fruitful?" holding out his shoe, asked them whether it was not new and well made. "Yet," added he, "none of you can tell where it pinches me."

PLUTARCH

Love matches, as they are called, have illusion for their father and need for their mother.

FRIEDRICH NIETZSCHE

The wooing should be a day after the wedding.

JOHN LYLY

The first wife from God; the second from man; the third from the devil.

POLISH PROVERB

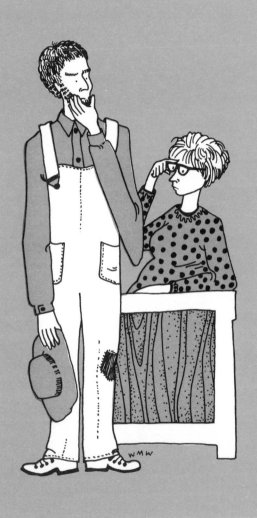

It is easier to be a lover than a husband, for the simple reason that it is more difficult to have a ready wit the whole day long than to say a good thing occasionally.

HONORÉ DE BALZAC

In the long run it is with a profession as with a marriage, we cease to remark anything but its drawbacks.

HONORÉ DE BALZAC

Before going to war say a prayer; before going to sea say two prayers; before marrying say three prayers.

PROVERB

Marriage is a noose often endured around the neck, but seldom endured around the feet.

PROVERB

The trouble with a marriage license is that it doesn't expire every year as other licenses do.

They dream in courtship, but in wedlock wake.

ALEXANDER POPE

Oh! a maid is charming sometimes, but a widow always.

PROVERB

A reformed rake makes the best husband.

PROVERB

He who lives without quarreling is a bachelor.

ST. JEROME

Brevity is the soul of widowhood.

SAKI

It isn't tying himself to one woman that a man dreads when he thinks of marrying; it's separating himself from all the others.

HELEN ROWLAND

Commend a wedded life, but keep thyself a bachelor.

PROVERB

The innkeeper loves a drunkard, but not for his son-in-law.

PROVERB

Advice to persons about to marry:
—Don't.

PUNCH

Never rely on the glory of the morning or on the smile of your mother-in-law.

ENGLISH PROVERB

The woman who resembles us is antipathetic: what we seek in the other sex is the opposite of ourselves.

RENAN

To love someone is to be the only one to see a miracle invisible to others.

FRANÇOIS MAURIAC

It is not a lack of love, but a lack of friendship that makes unhappy marriages.

FRIEDRICH NIETZSCHE

Love requires not so much proofs, as expressions of love. Love demands little else than the power to feel and to requite love.

JEAN PAUL RICHTER

An expensive wife makes a pensive husband.

PROVERB

In lovers' quarrels, the party that loves
most is always most willing to
acknowledge the greater fault.

SIR WALTER SCOTT

The good or ill hap of a good or ill life,
is the good or ill choice of a good or ill
wife.

SCOTTISH PROVERB

For a wife no poison is so bitter as when
her husband tells her that another
woman's skin is fair.

JOAQUIN SETANTI

For yesterday is but a dream,
And tomorrow is only a vision;
But today, well-lived,
Makes every yesterday
A dream of happiness,
And every tomorrow a vision of hope.

FROM THE SANSKRIT

A maid marries to please her parents; a widow to please herself.

WILLIAM SCARBOROUGH

In their hearts, women think that it is men's business to earn money and theirs to spend it—if possible during their husband's life, but, at any rate, after his death.

ARTHUR SCHOPENHAUER

In our part of the world where monogamy is the rule, to marry means to halve one's rights and double one's duties.

ARTHUR SCHOPENHAUER

We never live so intensely as when we love strongly. We never realize ourselves so vividly as when we are in the full glow of love for others.

WALTER RAUSCHENBUSCH

Love comforteth like sunshine after rain.

WILLIAM SHAKESPEARE

A light wife doth make a heavy
husband.

WILLIAM SHAKESPEARE

Men are April when they woo,
December when they wed: maids are
May when they are married, but the sky
changes when they are wives.

WILLIAM SHAKESPEARE

When I said, I would die a bachelor, I
did not think I should live till I were
married.

WILLIAM SHAKESPEARE

For whom does the blind man's wife
paint herself?

ENGLISH PROVERB

When a marriage ends in divorce, it is merely another fight that hasn't gone the distance.

Marriage is popular because it combines the maximum of temptation with the maximum of opportunity.

GEORGE BERNARD SHAW

It's a woman's business to get married as soon as possible, and a man's to keep unmarried as long as he can.

GEORGE BERNARD SHAW

A married man forms married habits and becomes dependent on marriage just as a sailor becomes dependent on the sea.

GEORGE BERNARD SHAW

He who is tired of a quiet life gets him a wife.

SPANISH PROVERB

God save us from all wives who are angels in the streets, saints in the church, and devils at home.

C. H. SPURGEON

On Saturday night last a gentlewoman's husband strayed from the playhouse in the Haymarket. If the lady who was seen to take him up will restore him, she shall be asked no questions; he being of no use but to the owner.

RICHARD STEELE

The lover thinks oftener of reaching his mistress than does the husband of guarding his wife; the prisoner thinks oftener of escaping than does the jailer of shutting the door.

STENDHAL

Marriage is one long conversation, chequered by disputes.

ROBERT LOUIS STEVENSON

What God hath joined together no man
shall ever put asunder: God will take
care of that.

GEORGE BERNARD SHAW

A married man can do anything he likes
if his wife don't mind. A widower can't
be too careful.

GEORGE BERNARD SHAW

Familiar acts are beautiful through love.

PERCY BYSSHE SHELLEY

Many waters cannot quench love,
neither can floods drown it.

SONG OF SOLOMON 8:7

If we take matrimony at its lowest, we
regard it as a sort of friendship
recognized by the police.

ROBERT LOUIS STEVENSON

A man always chases a woman until she catches him.

The heart of a coquette is like a rose, of which the lovers pluck the leaves, leaving only the thorns for the husband.

A husband is simply a lover with a two-days' growth of beard, his collar off, and a bad cold in his head.

Marriage, which makes two one, is a lifelong struggle to discover which is that one.

June is the month of weddings and cooing. The billing follows.

A misunderstood husband is one whose wife really knows him.

UNKNOWN

All men are born free, but some get married.

UNKNOWN

No woman can satisfactorily explain to herself why she married her husband.

UNKNOWN

A bachelor is a souvenir of some woman who found a better one at the last minute.

UNKNOWN

The reason why so few marriages are happy is because young ladies spend their time in making nets, not in making cages.

JONATHAN SWIFT

Love is having somebody to nudge
when you see something you like and
want to share it.

UNKNOWN

The game of love cannot be played with
the cards on the table.

Marriage is a covered dish.

SWISS PROVERB

Three weeks are passed in joint
examination, three months in love, then
come three years of dispute, thirty years
of toleration, and the children begin over
again.

HIPPOLITE TAINE

When a divorced man marries a divorced
woman, there are four minds in the bed.

TALMUD

Any and every intimate relation that is not based on love is a profanation of the flesh.

SUZANNE VOILQUIN

Marriage is the only adventure open to the cowardly.

VOLTAIRE

The husband who desires to surprise is often very much surprised himself.

VOLTAIRE

We love best in the days when we believe that we alone love, that no one has ever loved like us and no one ever will.

JOHANN WOLFGANG VON GOETHE

Love concedes in a moment what we can hardly attain by effort after years of toil.

JOHANN WOLFGANG VON GOETHE

God did not create woman from man's head, that he should command her, nor from his feet, that she should be his slave, but rather from his side, that she should be near his heart.

THE TALMUD

Choose a wife rather by your ear than your eye.

ENGLISH PROVERB

When the wife drinks to the husband all is well.

ENGLISH PROVERB

To love a person means to agree to grow old with him.

ALBERT CAMUS

I have lived long enough to know that the evening glow of love has its own riches and splendour.

BENJAMIN DISRAELI